Find Names
for the Temple

A Step-by-Step Method for Success

Find Names
for the Temple

A Step-by-Step Method for Success

Nicole Dyer with Diana Elder, AG

FAMILY
LOCKET
BOOKS

PUBLISHED BY
Family Locket Books, an imprint of
Family Locket Genealogists LLC
Highland, Utah

The views expressed in this book are those of the author and do not necessarily represent those of the International Commission for the Accreditation of Professional Genealogists (ICAPGen) or the Church of Jesus Christ of Latter-day Saints.

The International Commission for the Accreditation of Professional Genealogists, internationally recognized by its proprietary service mark, ICAPGen℠, owns the registered certification marks AG® and Accredited Genealogist. Genealogists who meet the competency standards established by ICAPGen are given a limited license to use the certification marks in connection with the providing of genealogical and historical research services.

ISBN 978-1-7321881-1-2
Made in the United States of America

To my dear husband Lance Dyer and our cute descendants

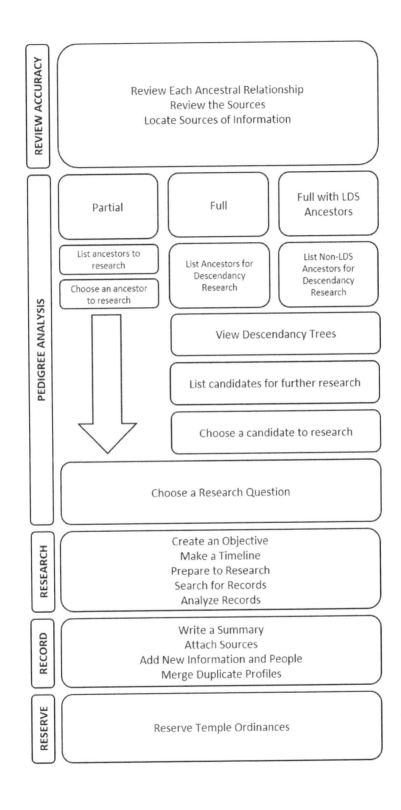

Contents

Foreword

Serving as a temple and family history consultant for several years, I was often frustrated when trying to help youth and adults find relatives who needed temple ordinances. Their trees were often seemingly full, but after an hour or so of clicking around in the *FamilySearch Family Tree* I could generally help them find a new individual or family.

They would happily go on their way with their temple cards ready for trek or youth conference or a family reunion. I knew though, that they had no idea how to repeat the steps on their own. They didn't know which ancestors we had started descendancy research with or how they were related to the cousins whose names we reserved for the temple.

I often wished I could send a person home with a systematic step-by-step process to work through their family tree and find names for the temple. They needed to learn a method for choosing ancestors for descendancy research. Then they needed to discover how to do a research project to verify identity and relationships. Finally, they needed a way to track their progress.

When Nicole shared her method for finding names for the temple, I knew this it was needed by every member of the Church of Jesus Christ of Latter-Day Saints.

I have found great joy in searching out my ancestors and I'm excited to recommend this method to others who want to experience the joy of temple and family history work.

-Diana Elder, Accredited Genealogist

Introduction

If your family tree is full or you are just getting started in family history research, you may be unsure about where to start. For many people, finding names for the temple is a challenging task!

When I served as a family history consultant, I helped youth and adults find research opportunities and prepare names for the temple. Some warned me that I was facing an uphill battle. Their family history had already been done. They believed their trees were full and that there were no research opportunities left. As I worked on these seemingly full family trees, I developed a system for discovering new branches of their tree. After adding these newly found relatives to *FamilySearch*, we reserved their names for temple work.

If you are willing to put in some time, effort, and prayer, you too can find branches of your family that are undiscovered and waiting for temple ordinances.

This book will help you know where to start and then guide you through the entire process. You'll review the accuracy of your tree, analyze your pedigree and choose a branch to research, perform genealogy research, record what you find, then reserve temple ordinances. After you've successfully found names for the temple, you can repeat the process.

First, you'll review the accuracy of your tree. This step provides a firm foundation for all the research you do afterward. You don't want to start researching a line that hasn't been confirmed and is not correct. You could end up researching someone else's ancestors and cousins!

Second, you will analyze your pedigree. You'll decide if your tree is partial or full. Then, if your tree is full, you will carefully and systematically go through your family tree to find your ancestors who were the first to join the Church of Jesus Christ of Latter-day Saints and make a list of their nonmember parents. You will pay special attention to these nonmember ancestors and their relatives like siblings, aunts and uncles, and children. These family members who did not join the church are sometimes under-researched and have incomplete families in *FamilySearch*.

In the third chapter, you will view descendancy trees using the free *Puzzilla* descendancy tree viewer and *FamilySearch Family Tree* in descendancy view. As you find gaps in these descendancy trees, you will choose a branch to research.

Fourth, you will research your selected branch. You'll learn about the location where your relatives lived and how to conduct genealogy research there. You'll review what is already known about that relative by looking carefully at the sources attached to them in *FamilySearch*, then make a timeline about their life. You will then make a research plan listing specific record collections, then search for records and keep track of what you find in a research log. After that, you will analyze the records to see if they match the relative you're researching and determine their accuracy.

The fifth chapter is about recording your findings by adding new details and people to *FamilySearch Family Tree* and writing reason statements. You may even want to write a research report, a life sketch, or notes about what you learned.

Next, you will reserve temple ordinances and print ordinance cards. Now you are ready to go to the temple. There's a special kind of joy that comes from bringing names of relatives you researched yourself to the temple.

Chapter Seven is about how to continue the process. The next time you need to find more family names for the temple, you will repeat the steps. Using the lists and notes that you've made, you can easily go back and select more branches to research. As you go through your tree systematically and keep a record of what you've done, you'll know what to do next.

If you have questions along the way, I encourage you to go to FamilyLocket.com and read our "how to" articles. You can also look up your questions at the *FamilySearch* learning center or reach out to your local family history consultant or family history center. They will be able to walk you through the *FamilySearch* website and help with genealogy research strategies.

At some point, you may get stuck on a difficult research question. You might want to learn more about genealogy research to help you solve it. Our book *Research Like a Pro: A Genealogists Guide* could be just what you need to take your research to the next level. If you need professional help, feel free to reach out to us at Family Locket.com for a consultation. The first time you start doing family history research, you may feel overwhelmed. I hope that using this step-by-step process can reduce feelings of overwhelm and discouragement. Having a method to follow can give you hope that finding names for the temple is possible.

Start small and work on family history research regularly, at whatever interval your schedule permits. I have had great results by working for 30 minutes a day. Even one hour per week, when you keep track of where you are in the process, can produce wonderful results over time. By small and simple things are great things brought to pass (Alma 37:6). Remember that your family tree is unique. Don't compare your experience researching to the experiences of others.

Your small, regular efforts are like a gardener planting daffodil bulbs. Just as each bulb must be planted one at a time, our relatives must be researched and verified one at a time. Someday you will look back on your efforts and realize you have found hundreds of relatives.

In *The Daffodil Principle*, Jaroldeen Asplund Edwards wrote about her visit to a five-acre daffodil field in Lake Arrowhead, California. She said,

> Before me lay the most glorious sight, unexpectedly and completely splendid. It looked as though someone had taken a great vat of gold and poured it down over the mountain peak and slopes where it had run into every crevice and over every rise. Even in the mist-filled air, the mountainside was radiant, clothed in massive drifts and waterfalls of daffodils. The flowers were planted in majestic, swirling patterns, great ribbons and swaths of

deep orange, white, lemon yellow, salmon pink, saffron,
and butter yellow.[1]

Jaroldeen couldn't imagine who could have planted the
thousands of bulbs in thirty-five different varieties. Then she
read the poster hanging on the porch of a nearby home.

> Answers to the Questions I Know You Are Asking
>
> 50,000 bulbs.
>
> One at a time, by one woman, two hands, two feet, and
> very little brain.
>
> Began in 1958.

Seeing the daffodil field and reading the poster was a life-
changing experience for Jaroldeen. She wrote,

> There it was. The Daffodil Principle.
>
> For me that moment was a life-changing experience. I
> thought of this woman whom I had never met, who,
> more than thirty-five years before, had begun — one
> bulb at a time — to bring her vision of beauty and joy to
> an obscure mountain top. One bulb at a time.
>
> There was no other way to do it. One bulb at a time.
> No shortcuts — simply loving the slow process of
> planting. Loving the work as it unfolded.

Instead of becoming discouraged at the seemingly slow work of
finding one person at a time, we can relish the process of
finding and getting to know our relatives one by one.

---

[1] Jaroldeen Asplund Edwards, *The Daffodil Principle* (Salt Lake City:
Shadow Mountain, 2004).

Just like ministering to a living person and helping them prepare for the temple, ministering to our deceased relatives and helping them along the covenant path requires time. We must get to know them. As we learn about them, record the details of their lives, and perform temple ordinances for them, we plant them in our hearts. As President Henry B. Eyring said, "You are not just gathering names. Those you never met in life will become friends you love. Your heart will be bound to theirs forever."[2]

After years of gathering our relatives, someday we too can look back on the many names we have found as a beautiful field that we have planted "one at a time." Each ancestor or relative that we find and add to our family tree is important to Heavenly Father. He wants us to remember the worth of each one of them. Doctrine and Covenants 18:10, 15-16 reads,

> The worth of souls is great in the sight of God; And if it so be that you should labor all your days in crying repentance unto this people, and bring, save it be *one soul* unto me, how great shall be your joy with him in the kingdom of my Father.
> And now, if your joy will be great with *one soul* that you have brought unto me in the kingdom of my Father, how great will be your joy if you should bring many souls unto me!

In the work of salvation, ministering, missionary work, and temple and family history work are one great work. The work of salvation is about seeking the one that is lost. In his book *One by*

---

[2] Henry B. Eyring, "Hearts Bound Together," April 2005 General Conference, article online, *LDS.org* (www.lds.org/general-conference : accessed 28 June 2018).

One, Elder David A. Bednar discusses the importance of ministering one by one. He shared the following quote from Elder Joseph B. Wirthlin's talk, "Concern for the One."

> Jesus Christ is our greatest example. He was surrounded by multitudes and spoke to thousands, yet He always had concern for the one. "For the Son of man is come to save that which was lost," He said. "What man of you, having an hundred sheep, if he lose one of them, doth not leave the ninety and nine in the wilderness, and go after that which is lost, until he find it?"

> This instruction applies to all who follow Him. We are commanded to seek out those who are lost. We are to be our brother's keeper. We cannot neglect this commission given by our Savior. We must be concerned for the one.[3]

It may seem like searching for ancestors one by one will take more time than we have. Yet President Russell M. Nelson has encouraged us to "prayerfully consider what kind of sacrifice – preferably a sacrifice of time – [we] can make [to] do more temple and family history work."[4]

In my personal experience, sacrificing time for family history and temple work has brought great blessings, including and heavenly help in other areas of my life. The time I have spent

---

[3] Joseph B. Wirthlin, "Concern for the One," April 2008 General Conference, article online, *LDS.org* (www.lds.org/general-conference : accessed 28 June 2018) quoted in David A. Bednar, *One by One* (Salt Lake City: Deseret Book, 2017).
[4] Russell M. Nelson and Wendy W. Nelson, "Open the Heavens through Temple and Family History Work," Liahona, October 2017; article online, *LDS.org* (www.lds.org/liahona : accessed 28 June 2018).

searching for my ancestors has been delightful. I can say with Elder Richard G. Scott that "it will make you feel wonderful."[5]

I want to invite you to join our Facebook Group, Find Names for the Temple. In the group, you can share your progress and get help from others in the group as your work through the Find Names for the Temple process. Just go to Facebook.com and search "Find Names for the Temple." Then select the group and ask to join.

-Nicole

---

[5] Richard G. Scott, "The Joy of Redeeming the Dead," October 2012 General Conference; article online, LDS.org (www.lds.org/general-conference : accessed 28 June 2018).

1

Review the Accuracy of Your Tree

Are you read to get started? Open your *FamilySearch* account and look at your family tree. It is essential to ensure the links in your family tree are correct before beginning a research project to find names for the temple. Temple work should only be completed for one's own relatives.

It is possible to unknowingly research and submit names for people who are not your relatives. You can avoid this by reviewing your family tree for accuracy and selecting relatives to research whose relationship to you has been confirmed.

For example, your tree is full and you decide to choose an ancestral couple and do descendancy research to find their children and grandchildren. If you choose distant ancestral couple whose relationship to you has not been proven through original records, you may spend hours searching for cousins that are actually not related to you. An original record is the first record created of an event, for example, a birth certificate, census record, or a will and probate record. Read more about original records in Chapter Four, "Research."

FamilySearch Family Tree is a collaborative family tree. You may not know how other contributors came to their conclusions. This is why it is important to review the relationships in your family tree to make sure you agree with the conclusions and the ancestors who have been added.

Below are some basic steps to do this. It may be helpful during this process to print a fan chart to keep track of who you have reviewed. Once you confirm that the parent-child relationship looks correct, you can check them off. For those who you cannot confirm, add a question mark or make a note to return to that ancestor later.

Review Each Ancestral Relationship

Start with yourself and work your way back to your great-grandparents. If you don't have firsthand knowledge of these relationships, ask your close relatives. Your grandparents or other relatives may have added "memories" to *FamilySearch* which contain biographies and life sketches of ancestors. A story can be used to help determine accuracy of a parent-child relationship when it is a firsthand account. For example, if your great-aunt adds memories about her grandmother, this is a firsthand account confirming the relationship between a known relative and your great-great grandmother who you did not know.

Review the Sources

Once you have traced your tree backward to ancestors who cannot be confirmed by memory, review the sources attached to *FamilySearch* to determine the accuracy of the parent-child relationships.

FamilySearch Family Tree has a section for sources in each profile. Click on every source and read the transcription and reason statement telling why it was attached. Click on the image and read the actual document.

For example, I have been told about my great grandmother, Ettie Belle Harris. I also have a picture of Ettie and her mother, Alice Frazier, so I know Alice is my ancestor. However Alice's parents' names, Richard Frazier and Nancy Elizabeth Briscoe, are not familiar to me. To make sure the information in *FamilySearch Family Tree* is correct, I reviewed the sources attached to Alice Frazier and her family to see if they accurately show that Alice's parents are Richard Frazier and Nancy Elizabeth Briscoe. Here's what I found:

- 1900 Census: Alice Frazier is listed as "daughter" of Richard Frazier and Nancy E. Frazier. Several siblings to Alice are also listed. This seems to match what is listed in FamilySearch.
- No marriage record was attached to Richard Frazier and Nancy E. Briscoe.
- A death record for one of Alice's brothers lists his parents' names as "Richard Frazier and Nancy Brisco."

The evidence in the 1900 census and the death record of Alice's brother make it clear to me that Alice Frazier is the daughter of Richard Frazier and Nancy Elizabeth Briscoe, so I'm ready to move on.

Now I want to check Nancy Elizabeth Briscoe's relationship to her parents, who are listed in *FamilySearch Family Tree* as John

Briscoe and Susannah Clanton. In the sources attached to them, this is what I found:

- In the 1850 census, "Nancy Briscoe" is living in the household of John Briscoe, age 56, and Susana Briscoe, age 33. There were six total children, ages 3-13. Nothing in the census explicitly says Nancy is their daughter but it does look like a family group of two parents and six children.
- There are no marriage records attached to John Briscoe and Susannah Clanton, but their estimated marriage date is given as 1835 in Tennessee.
- In the death certificate of one of the sons, his mother's maiden name is given as "Clanton."

After checking the sources, I am satisfied that this research is correct, and that Nancy Elizabeth Briscoe's parents are indeed John Briscoe and Susannah Clanton. I will put a checkmark next to their names in my notes.

Susannah Clanton's parents are listed in *FamilySearch* as John Clanton and Mrs. John Clanton. I want to check the evidence for this parent-child relationship now. Here is what I notice in the sources attached to Susannah and her supposed parents:

- There are only two sources attached to Susannah Clanton - one is the 1850 census in which she appears as an adult in the household of John Briscoe, her husband. The other is a death record for one of her sons.
- John Clanton has three censuses attached to him: the 1820, 1830, and 1840 census, in which his name is the only listed and the other household members are tick marks.

- The family group shows that five children were born to John Clanton and his first wife, name unknown, and then he remarried a woman named Sarah and had eight more children.

This is not enough evidence to confirm the parent-child relationship between Susannah Clanton and her proposed father, John Clanton. I would like to do more research to determine if this is correct. For now, I will put a question mark next to John Clanton's name and consider this as a possible research avenue in the future.

Locate Sources of Information

If there are no sources attached to one of your ancestors, this is a clue that they have not been thoroughly researched or the research was not shared on *FamilySearch Family Tree.* There are several things you can do to determine which sources the information came from.

- Contact the *FamilySearch* users who are listed in the recent changes of your ancestor's profile and ask for the sources they used.
- Look for research that has already been shared on other family tree sharing sites. These include *Ancestry, MyHeritage, Wiki Tree, RootsWeb, FindMyPast,* etc.
- Research the person to find original records. If you decide to do this, go to Chapter Four.

Tools That Help

When in landscape, portrait, and descendancy views, *FamilySearch Family Tree* displays icons next to relatives who have record hints, research suggestions, or data problems. You can use these icons to help you determine the accuracy of relationships. For example, if your sixth great grandfather is showing the red data problems icon, click the icon to learn more. The message might read, "Birth before father could have children: the child's birth year occurs before the father was at least 12." Review the sources and evidence between this child and father before proceeding to research beyond this relationship.

2

Analyze Your Pedigree

Who is missing from your family tree? The next step in finding names for the temple is to analyze your family tree and determine what you do and don't know. You'll find gaps in your family tree that can lead to finding new relatives. If you have a partial tree, the gaps will be obvious. You might have a great-grandfather whose parents are unknown. Maybe you don't have the name of your great-great grandmother.

If you have a full tree, you may not see where the gaps are. It will take more effort to find branches that are missing, especially if you have many early Latter-day Saint ancestors.

Partial Tree

Those who are just beginning to research their family history may only know about their grandparents and great-grandparents. Maybe you know a lot about your mother's side, but your father's side is empty. This is a partial family tree. A partial family tree is missing some or all the direct ancestors within the first four generations.

Choosing someone to focus on in a partial tree is simple. Look at your fan chart and make a list of each ancestor who is missing parents.

You may also want to make a list of ancestors whose siblings are missing. Finding the siblings of your ancestors is a wonderful way to find names for the temple.

Look at your lists and prayerfully choose an ancestor to focus on. After you have chosen an ancestor to start with, create a research question. For example, "Who are the parents of George Welch?" Now you are ready to proceed to Chapter Four, "Research."

If your research question focuses on a close relative, like a parent or grandparent, it will be most fruitful to gather information from relatives first. Recent sources are protected by privacy laws and you may need to prove that you are a son or daughter of the person whose records you are ordering.

Once you have discovered more ancestors and your family tree becomes full to the point that it is becoming difficult to find new ancestors, proceed to the next section for suggestions about finding research opportunities when your tree is full.

Full Tree

A full family tree is filled out with at least four generations or more. You have found all the ancestors that you can, including their siblings. Now you are stuck. When the research to find new ancestors is difficult, it is time to begin descendancy research.

Descendancy research is the process of choosing an ancestral couple and finding their children, grandchildren, great-grandchildren, and so forth. In this method, you are searching for your distant cousins who need temple ordinances.

Before beginning descendancy research, you will make a list of ancestors who lived long enough ago to be good starting points for descendancy research. Be sure that you have reviewed the accuracy of your tree and that the relationship between you and each ancestor is confirmed through original records. If you have many early Latter-day Saint ancestors and most of the people in your tree were also members during their life, skip to the next section about choosing a nonmember branch to research.

List Ancestors for Descendancy Research

If your family tree is full and most of your ancestors were not members of the Church of Jesus Christ of Latter-day Saints, the next step is to make a list of ancestors who are good starting points for descendancy research. An ancestor is a good starting point if they were born long enough ago that they will have descendants to discover that are eligible for temple ordinances. These descendants must have been born more than 110 years ago to be eligible for temple ordinances without permission from their closest living relative. For example, in the year 2018, you must choose an ancestor born in 1908 or before to reserve their temple work without permission.

Because of this 110-year rule, the descendancy research process will work best when you choose an ancestor born before 1820 as the starting point. They will have more descendants to research who were born before 1908 or whatever year is the current cutoff.

Take a systematic approach to creating your list of ancestors for descendancy research. Start with your paternal grandfather's ancestors, then your paternal grandmother's, and so on.

My Grandpa Shults was the first person in his family to join the Church. None of his ancestors were members. When I first started doing family history research about fifteen years ago, his family tree was partial. Now that my mother and I have filled out his tree more, it is getting full, and to find names for the temple on his side of the family, I need to do descendancy research. I created the table shown below to list his ancestors who were born before 1820 to keep track of which descendancy trees I have researched.

List of Ancestors for Descendancy Research

Ancestors of:	Grandpa Shults			
Name	ID	Notes (Birth Year, etc.)	# of Targets in 4 generations	Candidates for Further Research
Hickman Monroe Shults	2MKF-ZDD	b. 1820		
Rachel Cox	L7K9-4L3	b. 1827		
Barnet Isenhower	KN1G-XD8	b. 1821		
Mary Ann Pointer	LHH9-NNC	b. 1829		
Thomas Beverly Royston	KFR2-8KY	b. 1806		
Cynthia Dillard	KZ5B-X3X	b. 1816		
William H. Weatherford	2MJW-73V	b. 1815		
Mary "Clemsy" Cline	K2N9-RT9	b. 1818		
James Benjamin Harris	K2FZ-3VQ	b. 1819		
Martha Hooser	KDSW-YXK	b. 1821		
George Welch	L8Q2-VDT	b. 1802		
Lucindrilla Keaton	L8Q2-VXZ	b. 1805		

James Jackson Frazier	KLND-PYW	b. 1815		
Gloria Isabell McChristian	KLND-KQM	b. 1817		
John Briscoe	L441-67X	b. 1817		
Susannah Clanton	K2ND-FK6	b. 1817		

A template for this table is included in the appendix. To fill out your own table, log in to the *FamilySearch Family Tree* and view the tree in the fan chart view. Make separate lists for your paternal grandfather, then your paternal grandmother, maternal grandfather, and finally maternal grandmother, unless you are just focusing on one particular grandparents' ancestors like I did. Put him or her in the center of the fan chart by clicking on the gray bar under his or her name. You should now see five generations of your family tree, starting with your grandparent.

Start with the bottom left of your fan chart and find the first ancestor who was born before 1820. Move across your fan chart from left to right. List each ancestor who was born before about 1820.

In the example above, most of the ancestors listed were born before 1820. They are the great-great-grandparents of my Grandpa Shults, in the outer ring of his fan chart.

Now that you have a list of starting points for descendancy research, proceed to the next chapter about descendancy tree analysis to continue filling out your table. Once you have completed this table, you will have a list of candidates to research and find spouses and children who are missing from the family tree.

List Nonmember Ancestors for Descendancy Research

Those with many early members of the Church in their family tree may find it difficult to find a starting place for descendancy research. For example, if you choose an ancestor who was a member of the Church as a starting point for descendancy research, you may find that many of their children and grandchildren were also members and do not need temple ordinances. So, in this section, you will learn how to find a nonmember branch of your family tree to research.

The first step is to determine who in your family tree was a member, and who was not. Then, you'll make a list of all the nonmember branches or family lines in your family tree.

To help you keep track of these family lines, create a list in a table or spreadsheet. You can use the table in the appendix or create your own. I suggest creating a separate list for each grandparent. Three of my grandparents have early Latter-day Saint ancestors, so I created a list for each of them. This helps me easily remember which side of the family I'm researching.

Print a fan chart of each of your grandparents' ancestors. Annotating these fan charts will help you keep track of where you are as you determine which ancestors were members and which were not.

Starting with your paternal grandfather's chart, put dots next to everyone who you know was a member. When you get to someone you're not sure about, use the clues on the next pages to determine if he or she joined the Church or not. Go back in your family tree until you reach the first ancestor who was not a member.

Circle their name on the printed fan chart and add them to your list. Include their *FamilySearch* ID number and in the column for notes, list the names of their children who did join the Church. You will need this later, especially if more than one child joined the Church.

To determine which children joined the Church, open the person page of your ancestor in a new tab and look at each of their children's person cards. Use the clues described on the next pages to determine which children joined the Church. Often only your direct ancestor joined the Church.

Clue: Birth and Death Places

Check the place of birth and death. Most early members of the Church migrated away from their birthplace and died in Utah, Arizona, Idaho, or Nevada (the Intermountain West) in the 1800s. Some early members also died along the pioneer trail (Wyoming, Nebraska, etc.) or in other early Latter-day Saint settlements (Winter Quarters, Nauvoo, Illinois, Missouri, Ohio, etc.).

Ancestors who did not join the Church stayed closer to their birthplace. Their birth and death places will probably be in Europe or the Eastern United States. Perhaps they migrated to states other than the Intermountain West.

In the *FamilySearch Family Tree* fan chart view, click on your ancestor's name to view their person card to quickly look at their birthplace and deathplace. Here are some examples.

Example #1: Mariah Brockhouse
      Birth: 1842 in Willenhall, Staffordshire, England
      Death: 1926, Springville, Utah
      Was this ancestor a member of the Church? **Probably.**

Example #2: Peder Jensen Rigtrup
>Birth: 1807, Randers, Arhus, Denmark
>Death: 1857, Omaha, Douglas, Nebraska
>Was this ancestor a member of the Church? **Possibly.**
>*Death date and place could have occurred during Mormon Pioneer migration. Omaha was along the Mormon trail. Check baptism date to be sure.*

Example #3: Mary Hargreaves
>Birth: 1789 Haslingden, Lancashire, England
>Death: 1847, Chorley, Lancashire, England
>Was this ancestor a member of the Church? **Not likely.**
>*Mary was born in England and died in England. She probably did not join the Church. Her parents, siblings and some of her children may be nonmember branches to research. Check her baptism date to confirm.*

Clue: Baptism and Confirmation Date

For further evidence about whether a person joined the Church or not, check their ordinance information. If the baptism occurred during their life, then they joined the Church during their life. If the baptism date is after their death date, then their baptism was performed in a temple by proxy, and it's almost certain they were not a member during their life.

In the *FamilySearch Family Tree* fan chart view, click on your ancestor's name to view their person card. Check the baptism date by hovering your mouse over the "B" in the temple section. A dialog box will appear with the date of baptism.

Example # 1: William Creer
>Born in Lancashire, England in 1836, died in Spanish Fork, Utah in 1900. Baptism completed in 1844. Was William Creer a member of the Church?

- Migrated to Utah
- Baptized during his life in 1844 at age 8

William Creer was a member of the Church during his life. I will need to go back to his parents or grandparents to find a nonmember ancestor.

Example # 2: Matthias Creer

Born 1791 in Whitehaven, Cumberland, England, died in 1857 in Preston, Lancashire, England. Baptism completed in 1879. Was Matthias a member of the Church?

- Did not migrate to the Intermountain West
- Baptism performed after his death

Matthias was not a member of the Church during his life. I will add his name to my list of nonmember ancestors.

Example # 3: Ann Miller

Born in Lincolnshire, England in 1805. Died in Spanish Fork, Utah Territory in 1865. Baptism completed in Salt Lake Temple on 2 May 1977. Confirmation completed on 20 June 1849. Initiatory completed at Endowment House on 8 March 1862. Was Ann Miller a member of the Church?

- Migrated England to Utah
- Baptism performed after her death
- Confirmation occurred during her life in 1849

Ann Miller was a member of the Church during her life. Although her baptism date is showing in *FamilySearch* as 1977 instead of the original baptism date, I noticed her confirmation and other ordinances were completed during her life.

Sometimes proxy baptisms were unknowingly repeated for early members of the Church after their death. FamilySearch should show the original baptism date, but if that original date of baptism has been lost, a proxy baptism date is shown.

Check the confirmation date and initiatory/endowment dates as well. Some ordinances for the dead were done in the endowment house before a temple was complete in Utah. The endowment house was operational from 1855-1889.

If you suspect an ancestor joined the Church during their life but their baptism date on *FamilySearch* appears to be after their death, check the memories section. Stories and biographies about early Latter-day Saint ancestors will often contain details about their conversion to the Church.

List of Nonmember Ancestors for Descendancy Research

Ancestors of:	Grandma Shults				
Name	**ID**	**Notes (Spouses names, children who joined the Church)**	**# of Targets in 4 generations**	**Candidates for Further Research**
Matthias Creer	LZ66-PLK	Married Nellie Greenhalgh. Children Edward and Catherine became Latter-day Saints.		
Nellie Greenhalgh	LZ66-PG7	Married to Matthias Creer, same as above.		
Robert Greenhalgh	L7G5-16S	Married Jane Taylor. Their daughter Nellie became Latter-day Saints.		
Jane Taylor	L7G5-12M	Jane married Robert Greenhalgh. Same as above.		

Above is an example from my list of nonmember ancestors. I included notes about their spouses and children who joined the Church. It's especially important to note if they were married more than once. This could mean that they have additional descendants with their other spouse.

After making a list of all the nonmember branches on your paternal grandfather's side of the family tree, repeat the process for each of your grandparents who have early Latter-day Saint ancestors.

In the next chapter you will create descendancy trees for each person in your list and continue filling out the table with research targets and candidates for further research.

3

Analyze Descendancy Trees

In the previous sections, you have verified the accuracy of your family tree, including connections to all your direct line ancestors. You have analyzed your family tree and made a list of ancestors for starting points in descendancy research.

Now you will view descendancy trees for each of the ancestors in your list. As you gather information about their descendants and notice research opportunities, you will continue to fill out the columns in your table with # of targets and candidates for further research.

View Descendancy Trees

There are two main ways to view a descendancy tree, *Puzzilla* and *FamilySearch Family Tree* descendancy view. Your own personal genealogy software may also have a descendancy view. A descendancy tree places an ancestor or ancestral couple at the top and lists their children, grandchildren, great-grandchildren, and so on. You can choose how many generations of descendants to view.

Puzzilla Descendancy Trees

Puzzilla is a FamilySearch partner app that allows you to view ancestry and descendancy family trees from a bird's eye view to find new research opportunities. Go to their website, *Puzzilla*.org, and sign in with your *FamilySearch* account. View the "how to" section to watch videos and how to use the website.

When you're ready to get started, go to the home page or click "chart." You will see a pedigree chart with yourself as the root person and six generations of ancestors. On the left, you can see the control panel with your name and *FamilySearch* ID number, the number of generations you are viewing, and a key explaining the colors in the chart.

To view the descendancy tree for the first ancestor on your list, go to the control panel and click "Change ID." Copy and paste the *FamilySearch* ID into the box and click "view descendants." A new window will open with a descendancy tree showing your ancestor at the center and his or her descendants circling around him in concentric circles. Each circle represents a new generation.

Puzzilla can highlight people in the descendancy tree who are recommended targets for research. The criteria for targets is a person who reached childbearing age but has no children listed in *FamilySearch*. These are not the only candidates for further research in your tree, but they are helpful starting points.

To view the recommended targets, select the "targets" button in the control panel. Then, to deselect the other features, click the "Died <16" and "Born < 110" buttons. This will help you see just the red targets. Now your tree will show red squares next to relatives who are recommended targets for research. Count or estimate the number of recommended targets. Record the number of targets on your list. This will help you see the size of the research project and how likely you will be to find candidates for further research in this descendancy tree.

Repeat this process and create *Puzzilla* descendancy trees for each of the ancestors in your list.

As you do so, you may notice that the descendancy tree of a person's spouse is identical. This is common. Unless they were married more than once and had different children with each spouse, a husband and wife will have identical descendancy trees. However, skipping the process of viewing the descendants of the spouse of your ancestor could cause you to miss out on possible research opportunities.

For example, on the next page is a table showing the nonmember ancestors of my maternal grandmother and the number of targets in each of their descendancy trees. As you can see, most ancestors were married just once and have the same descendancy trees as their spouses. I kept track of this in the "number of targets" column, simply typing "same as above" if the spouse's descendancy tree was the same.

In the example on the next page, Mary Miller and Edward Inckley are the ancestral couple in my family tree. However, they were not married when their daughter, Ann, was born. Edward was married to a different woman, so he and Mary Miller have completely different descendancy trees.

List of Nonmember Ancestors for Descendancy Research

Ancestors of:	Grandma Shults			
Name	**ID**	**Notes (Spouses names, children who joined the Church)**	**# of Targets in 4 generations**	**Candidates for Further Research**
Matthias Creer	LZ66-PLK	Married Nellie Greenhalgh. Children Edward and Catherine became Latter-day Saints.	About 25 (not including the branches of Edward and Catherine)	
Nellie Greenhalgh	LZ66-PG7	Married to Matthias Creer. Same as above.	Same as above	
Thomas Bradley	L4WF-LP6	Never married but had children with Ann Miller and Elizabeth Maidens. Ann Miller and their daughter Sarah Jane Miller joined the church.	33	
Mary Powderill Bradley	LCTL-7RS	Mother of Thomas Bradley. Had 2 children outside marriage with an unknown father. Later married William Tales.	9	
Mary Miller	M2X2-KXZ	Had a child with Edward Inckley but they were not married. Her daughter Ann Miller joined the church.	8	
Edward Inkley	LKHM-R51	Married Alice Parkinson and had a child with Mary Miller. Only his daughter Ann Miller joined the church.	About 20 in the 2nd generation, about 75 in the 3rd generation	

Too Many Targets to Count

If your ancestor has many known descendants, it might be difficult to count the number of targets in their *Puzzilla* descendancy tree. One strategy to overcome this is to hide specific branches of the tree. Your own branch of the tree, shown in yellow, might be very large and full of Latter-day Saint descendants. To hide this branch, click on the child who joined the Church so that you can see their person card. Then, in the control panel, click the "hide/show tree" button.

In the descendancy tree of Matthias Creer in my chart above, I hid two branches of the tree who had both joined the Church. Matthias' son Edward and daughter Catherine joined the Church. Edward's branch of the descendancy tree filled half of the circle. Catherine's filled one-third. When I hid both of these branches, the tree was generated again and I could easily count the research possibilities for the nonmember branches of the Creer family.

Should I Research the Latter-day Saint branches of my family tree?

Yes, you should research the Latter-day Saint branches of your family tree. Descendancy research can reveal that they are missing people also. There is less of a chance that you will find names for the temple while checking the descendants of Latter-day Saint relatives, but there is a chance. If you notice many recommended research targets in one of your member lines, look into it. It is possible that one of the children in that family tree did not continue as a member of the Church and their descendants have not received temple ordinances.

FamilySearch Descendancy View

Another way to view a descendancy tree is to use the *FamilySearch Family Tree* in descendancy view. Choose one of the ancestors on your list and find them in *Family Tree.* Click on them to view their family tree. Switch to descendancy view and you will see a page of up to four generations of descendants for that ancestral couple. You can choose how many generations you would like to view at a time. You can also click "options" to

show or hide the portraits. If you hide the portraits, your descendancy view will be more compact.
One of the benefits of using *FamilySearch* descendancy view is seeing which relatives have data problems, research suggestions, and record hints. These brightly colored icons appear next to a person's name in *Family Tree.* This is helpful as you identify candidates for further research in the next step. A good candidate for further research has a research suggestion and record hint icons.

FamilySearch descendancy view also displays temple icons indicating if temple ordinances are ready to reserve. If you find ordinances ready to reserve in this step, verify the information and sources for your relative using the method in Chapter One, then reserve the ordinances.

List Candidates for Further Research

Now that you have viewed two kinds of descendancy trees and counted the targets in the *Puzzilla* tree, it's time to make a list of candidates for further research. Not all the targets you have counted will be good candidates, and not all good candidates will be marked as a recommended research target, but the targets are still a good place to start.

There are several things to look at when determining if someone is a candidate for further research. If they meet the qualifications below, add them to your table in the column "candidates for further research."

How to Determine a Candidate for Further Research
A person is a good candidate for further research if:

- they lived in a place where you can read and understand the language on the records (i.e. if you can't read Danish, you probably won't be able to research ancestors born in Denmark until you learn more about Danish research).

- they lived in a time when records are available (generally, there are not many records available to research before 1600 in most localities)

- enough information is already known about the person so that he or she can be uniquely identified (i.e. a name, at least one date and place)

- *FamilySearch* has already found record hints that might be a match, as shown in the top right portion of the *FamilySearch* person page called "Research Help"

- they lived long enough that they could have been married; and/or reached childbearing age

- the person's spouse is already known so you just need to find their children

A person will *not* be a good candidate for further research if they died before they reached childbearing age. Another reason a person would not be a good candidate for further research is if they have been well researched with many sources attached but none of the sources show they were married and had children (i.e. someone who stayed single their entire life).

A good candidate for further research lived in a time when records are available. So how can you know if there are records available in a certain time and place? To learn about the place you are considering researching, go to the *FamilySearch Wiki* (https://www.familysearch.org/wiki/en/Main_Page). Look up the country or state where your relative lived and see if there are any record collections in the correct time frame. Once you have become familiar with a specific country and the usual records used for research, you may not need to look up that country or region each time. For example, those familiar with research in the United States in the late 1800s know that census, state birth and death registration, and marriage records are some of the most common records used in genealogy research.

Research Hints

The research hints in the *FamilySearch* descendancy view can be especially valuable when trying to find candidates for further research. If you find someone who has no spouse or children, but a record hint for a census and a marriage record, you know you have found the perfect candidate. It can also be helpful to see an orange temple icon indicating that temple ordinances are needed but more information is required.

Puzzilla descendancy trees make it easier to visualize how many children are in each generation, but it doesn't allow you to see record hints if you are using the free version. You must click through to *FamilySearch* to view them.

In your *Puzzilla* descendancy tree, click on each of the targets you counted earlier. This opens a person card. Click "view in family tree." This opens their person page at *FamilySearch* in a new tab. You can then see if the person has any research hints at the top left of their person page.

For example, in the table on the next page, I viewed each of the nine research targets in the *Puzzilla* descendancy tree of Mary Powderill Bradley. Of these nine, I added three research candidates to my list. The first candidate had several research hints, which I noted.

Nonmember Ancestors of:	Grandma Shults			
Name	ID	Notes (Spouses names, children who joined the Church)	# of Targets in 4 gener-ations	Candidates for Further Research
Mary Powderill Bradley	LCTL-7RS	Several of the children of Elizabeth Miller and Ben Gregory only had 1-2 children.	9	- Pearce Sumter Bradley, LZVF-QNP, 3 record hints, record availability for England in the 1800s is good, and his wife is already listed. - George Gregory, K2NK-ZMB, appears as a 26-year-old in the 1901 census. He may get married and have children by the 1911 census. - Thomas Robert Maidens L62K-D1J, is found on the 1871 census as a child, but not again after that. Marriage and census records are available in the late 1800s.

The other six research targets in Mary Powderill Bradley's descendancy tree were not good candidates for further research. Here's why:

- Peggy Miller, born 1836 in England - I have already researched Peggy and cannot find any record of her existence except for a Mormon pioneer biography of her sister, Sarah Jane Miller Bradley, which I assume was written from family knowledge. Perhaps she died as a child.

- Sarah Ann Creer (1867-1946) - Sarah Ann has been well researched with many sources. The records show that she never married.

- Sarah Jane Miller (1871-1929) - Sarah Jane was also well researched, with a spouse listed, and several census records attached, all showing no children.

- Alfred George Miller (1863-?) - Alfred appears on the 1911 England census showing that he had been married for five years and his wife was the mother of no children. It appears that they both got married later in life.

- Tom Gregory (1862-1949) - Tom and his wife appear on the 1901 and 1911 England census with no children and in 1911, his wife is beyond childbearing years.

- Sarah Jane Gregory (1861-1935) - she appears on the 1911 England census at age 50 with no spouse or children.

Beyond the Research Targets

Some people who are not marked as a research target in a *Puzzilla* descendancy tree may still be good candidates for further research. For example, in Mary Powderill Bradley's *Puzzilla* descendancy tree, I noticed Mary Ellen Gregory. Only one child is showing for Mary Ellen, but she was not marked as a research target.

Only people who reached childbearing age and have *no* children are listed as research targets. It is possible that Mary Ellen Gregory had more than one child! I added her to my list of candidates for further research.

After you check each research target, look for other people in the *Puzzilla* descendancy tree who could be candidates for further research. They might be people who have just a few children listed and are missing censuses or other pertinent sources. Add these additional candidates for further research to your list.

Select a Candidate to Research

Now that you have several candidates to start researching, review your entire list and choose the most promising one. Follow the Spirit and choose a branch that has missing spouses, missing children, available records, and a language you are familiar with. Prayer can be a powerful help in deciding who to research. Elder Richard G. Scott said,

"This work is a spiritual work, a monumental effort of cooperation on both sides of the veil, where help is given in both directions. Anywhere you are in the world, with prayer, faith, determination, diligence, and some sacrifice, you can make a powerful contribution."[6]

Research Questions for Descendancy Research

After choosing a candidate, you should create a research question to guide your research. Create a separate research question for each person. Do the research for that one person, then move on to the next person. For example, if I am doing descendancy research and I want to find all the grandchildren of Richard Frazier, I would create a separate research question for each of his children. It is difficult to perform research for multiple families at once.

In the next chapter, we use your research question to create an objective. Generally, research questions in descendancy research will be asking for the spouse or children of a person. Here are some examples:

- Who are the children of Richard Frazier and Nancy Elizabeth Briscoe?

- Who is the spouse of John Frazier, son of Richard Frazier and Nancy Elizabeth Briscoe?

- Who are the children of Richard Frazier and Nancy Elizabeth Briscoe's son, John Frazier?

After you decide on a research question, you are ready to start a research project.

---

[6] Richard G. Scott, "The Joy of Redeeming the Dead," October 2012 General Conference; article online, *LDS.org* (www.lds.org/general-conference : accessed 28 June 2018).

4

Research

Create an Objective

Now that you have chosen a candidate for further research and a specific research question, it's time to create an objective for your research project. The objective should be narrow and specific. If your objective is too broad, your project may feel overwhelming and you may miss important details.

Generally, a narrow objective focuses on just one person. It usually focuses on their identity or their relationship to either parents, spouse, or children.

When starting this process for the first time, it is helpful to narrow your objective to a very specific piece of information you are seeking. After that is discovered, you can repeat the process again to find additional information. Here are some examples of broad and narrow research questions:

Example 1 - Florence Matilda Creer
- Broad: Who else is in the family of Florence Matilda Creer?

- Narrow: Who are the parents of Florence Matilda Creer?

Example 2 - The Bradleys
- Broad: Who are the grandchildren of Mary Powderill Bradley?
- Narrow: Who are the children of Pearce Sumpter Bradley?

Example 3 - Jane Baldock
- Broad: Who is Jane Baldock and who are her parents?
- Narrow: What is the birthdate and place of Jane Baldock?

As you can see above, the narrow objectives above are asking for specific information about a person's relationships or identity. Often in descendancy research, we are searching for the grandchildren and great-grandchildren of an ancestor. It is important, however, to break up this objective into smaller pieces. Focusing on just one person can help you concentrate on the small details in each source. These details often hold the answer your research question.

Next, add unique identifying information to your objective. These pieces of information will help you identify exactly you are researching and know if the records you find match or not.

The best unique identifiers are:
- Birthdate and place
- Marriage date and place
- Death date and place
- Spouse's name
- Parents' names

If none of this information is known, additional unique identifiers that can be used include:

- Residence date and place
- Another relative's name

Here are some examples of objectives with and without unique identifiers:

Example 1 - Florence Matilda Creer
- Without: Who are the parents of Florence Matilda Creer?
- With: Who are the parents of Florence Matilda Creer, born about 1892 in Utah and died 12 November 1977 in Burley, Cassia, Idaho, wife of Edward Raymond Kelsey, who she married on 14 November 1916 in Rupert, Minidoka, Idaho?

Example 2 - Pearce Sumpter Bradley
- Without: Who are the children of Pearce Sumpter Bradley?
- With: Who are the children of Pearce Sumpter Bradley, born 7 October 1821 to Mary Powderill Bradley in Swineshead, Lincolnshire, England, and married Jane Baldock, 8 February 1849, also in Swineshead?

Example 3 - Jane Baldock
- Without: What is the birthdate and place of Jane Baldock?
- With: What is the birthdate and place of Jane Baldock, who married Pearce Sumpter Bradley on 8 February 1849 in Swineshead, Lincolnshire, England?

Print your objective and put it in front of your computer as you research to help you know if a record matches your relative or not.

Make A Timeline

After you have created an objective with unique identifiers, you are ready to make a timeline. Gather everything that is known about the person and create a table or spreadsheet with the dates and places of events in their lives. Include dates and places of events for their immediate family also. Some examples include birth, baptism, marriage, residence, tax, land ownership, migration, etc. Use all the sources you have about the person and their family to help you gather facts for the timeline.

You should also include a column for the source of the information. During the creation of your timeline, you may have some questions or ideas. Write those down in the notes column.

Here is an example of a timeline for Pearce Sumpter Bradley:

Pearce Sumpter Bradley Timeline				
Objective:	Who are the children of Pearce Sumpter Bradley, christened 7 October 1821 in Swineshead, Lincolnshire, England, son of Mary Powderill Bradley, and married Jane Baldock, 8 February 1849, also in Swineshead?			
Event	**Date**	**Place**	**Source**	**Notes**
Baptism / Christening	7 Oct 1821	Swineshead, Lincolnshire, England	"England Births and Christenings, 1538-1975," database, *FamilySearch*	Pearce's birth record only lists his mother. Who is his father?

Mother Mary Bradley's marriage to William Tales	9 Dec 1829	Swineshead, Lincolnshire, England	"England Marriages, 1538–1973," database, FamilySearch	Indexed record - find the original record.
Residence	1841	Swineshead, Lincolnshire, England	"England and Wales Census, 1841," database with images, FamilySearch	Who is Benjamin Horn living with Pearce's family in 1841? Is he related to the family somehow?
Marriage to Jane Baldock	8 Feb 1849	Swineshead, Lincolnshire, England	"England Marriages, 1538–1973," database, FamilySearch	-Indexed record -Find an original record for Pearce and Jane's marriage to look for more clues. -What is Jane Baldock's birthdate and place? -If Pearce and Jane were married in 1849, they should appear on the 1851 Census as a married couple.

After you have created the timeline, make a list of all the places the person lived. Then choose the place that will most likely have the answer to your research question. You will learn more about this place in the next step. In my example, Pearce Bradley lived in Swineshead. I will learn more about that location in the next step.

Prepare to Research

Before you research, it is important to do some preparation. You will want to learn about the area where you will be researching and find out what records are available. You should also make a research plan and log.

Learn About the Location

Before looking for records about your relative, it is important to understand more about the location. In this step, you will look at maps, determine jurisdictions and boundary changes, and learn about record availability.

These are the main things you'll want to know:

1. What are the jurisdictions? A jurisdiction is a government or church entity that created records. They can be on different levels, i.e. state level, county level, etc. These are the places you will look for records.
   a. National
   b. State
   c. County
   d. City/township
   e. Church (i.e. parish, diocese)
   f. Civil registration district
2. What counties are nearby? These are additional places to look for records about your relative.
3. Were there any boundary changes in the country, state, or county?
4. When did record keeping begin for:
   a. Birth records
   b. Marriage records
   c. Death records
   d. Census records

A good place to start learning about locations is the *FamilySearch Wiki*. Go to https://familySearch.org/wiki and type in the place that you want to learn about. There are pages on the wiki for countries, states, counties, and some townships and cities. The Family History Guide also has a listing of resources by country at https://thefhguide.com/countries.html.

Additional online resources that can help you with historical geography include:

- FamilySearch Places
https://www.familysearch.org/research/places/
- England and Wales Jurisdictions
http://maps.familysearch.org
- The Atlas of Historical County Boundaries (U.S.)
http://publications.newberry.org/ahcbp/

There are many additional websites with information about localities including *Wikipedia, Google Books,* and the *Geographic Names Information System (GNIS).*

For example, in my research project to discover Pearce and Jane Bradley's children, I looked up the town where Pearce and Jane lived, Swineshead, at the *FamilySearch Wiki* and maps.familysearch.org. Then I and answered the four questions, adding additional jurisdictions and information where applicable.

Example: Swineshead, Lincolnshire, England

1. What are the jurisdictions?
   a. National: England
   b. State: not applicable
   c. County: Lincolnshire
   d. Town: Swineshead
   e. Church
      i. Parish: Swineshead (Church of England)
      ii. Rural Deanery: Holland
      iii. Diocese: Lincoln
      iv. Province: Canterbury
   f. Poor Law Union: Swineshead
   g. Hundred: Kirton
   h. Civil registration district: Boston

2. What towns or counties are nearby?
   a. Nearby parishes: Mown Rakes, Holland Fen, Frampton, Kirton in Holland, Sutterton, Wigtoft, Bicker, Great Hale, Fosdyke, Moulton, Surfleet, Gosberton, Quadring, Donington, Wyberton, Boston, Skirbeck, Pinchbeck, Spalding, Weston, Holbeach, South Kyme and North Kyme
   b. Nearby counties
      i. Bordering Lincolnshire: Yorkshire to the north, the North Sea to the east, Norfolk, Cambridgeshire, Northamptonshire, Rutlandshire, Leicestershire, and Nottinghamshire
      ii. Bordering the border counties: Durham, Westmorland, Lancashire, Cheshire, Derbyshire, Staffordshire, Warwickshire, Oxfordshire, Buckinghamshire, Bedfordshire, Huntingdonshire, Hertfordshire, Essex, Suffolk
3. Were there any boundary changes? - Not that I could find.
4. When did record keeping begin?
   a. Parish Registers: 1639
   b. Bishop's Transcripts: 1566
   c. Civil Birth/Marriage/Death Registration: July 1837
   d. Census: 1841

As you become more advanced, you will want to learn more about the history of the region you are researching as well. The more you understand the locality you are researching, the better you will become at finding records about your relatives.

You can also watch videos and webinars to help you understand the records that are available for certain places. Go to the *FamilySearch Help Center* to search their database of free articles, webinars, videos and other lessons. The URL is https://www.familysearch.org/ask/landing . From there, you can search for the place or record type you want to learn about. To narrow the results, click lessons. Then you will see a listing of videos and lessons to help you learn more.

Make a Research Plan and Log

After learning about the location and record availability of the place your relative lived, you should make a research plan. Keep the *FamilySearch Wiki* open. Make a list of all the sources you want to search to find the answer to your research question. You will find links to many record sets in the *FamilySearch Wiki*. Add these to your list. For example:

Ideas of record collections to search:
- England and Wales Calendar of Wills, 1858-1966, 1973-1995 at *Ancestry*
- 1851 Census at *Ancestry*
- 1861 Census at *Ancestry*
- 1871 Census at *Ancestry*
- 1881 Census at *Ancestry*
- Civil marriage registration at Lincolnshire Marriages website http://mi.lincolnshiremarriages.org.uk/
- England and Wales Christening Records, 1530-1906 at *Ancestry*
- Civil death registration at FreeBMD https://www.freebmd.org.uk/cgi/search.pl

Now that you have several ideas of record collections to search, create your research plan by making a list directly within the research log you will use. A research log helps you keep track of where you looked and what you found. You can use it to plan your research by listing the details of which record collections you want to search in the order you want to search them.

Start with the record collection you think will be most likely to contain the answer to your question or is a logical place to start tracing the family. When you do the searches, you will fill in the rest of your research log with the date and the results/notes.

For example, in my Pearce Bradley research project, I have prioritized my list of record collections to search in the research log below. I am looking for any children born to Pearce Bradley and his wife Jane, so I have chosen to search census and baptism records first.

Since I am looking for Pearce's children, it is logical to start with the 1851 census and follow the England census records every ten years to see if he and Jane had children. I decided not to search for the original image of Pearce's marriage yet, but perhaps I will do that later. Right now, the records that will best answer my research question are census and baptism records. Next, I will check probate records to see if Pearce Bradley left an inheritance to any children he had.

Research Plan and Log						
Objective:	Who are the children of Pearce Sumpter Bradley, christened 7 October 1821 in Swineshead, Lincolnshire, England, son of Mary Powderill Bradley, and married Jane Baldock, 8 February 1849, also in Swineshead?					
Date	**Website or Repository**	**URL, Call #, Film #**	**Searching for**	**Locality**	**Source**	**Results, Notes**
	Ancestry	https://search.ancestry.com/search/db.aspx?dbid=8860	Pearce Bradley and Jane	Swineshead, Lincolnshire	1851 England Census	
	Ancestry	https://search.ancestry.com/search/db.aspx?dbid=8767	Pearce Bradley and Jane	Swineshead, Lincolnshire	1861 England Census	
	Ancestry	https://search.ancestry.com/search/db.aspx?dbid=7619	Pearce Bradley and Jane	Swineshead, Lincolnshire	1871 England Census	

	Ancestry	https://search.ance stry.com/search/db .aspx?dbid=7572	Pearce Bradley and Jane	Swineshead, Lincolnshire	1881 England Census	
	Ancestry	https://search.ance stry.com/search/db .aspx?dbid=6598	Children of Pearce and Jane Bradley	Swineshead, Lincolnshire	1891 England Census	
	Ancestry	https://search.ance stry.co.uk/search/d b.aspx?dbid=1351	Children of Pearce and Jane Bradley	Swineshead, Lincolnshire	England & Wales Christening Index, 1530-1906	
	Ancestry	https://search.ance stry.com/search/db .aspx?dbid=1904	Will of Pearce Bradley	Swineshead, Lincolnshire	England & Wales, National Probate Calendar, 1858-1966, 1873-1995	

In a research log, there are many columns to record information about your search. Here is a description of each:

- **Date**: when you perform the search. Leave this blank while you make your research plan. After your plan is ready, start searching each collection and add the date you performed the search.

- **Website or Repository:** A repository is a place, building, or receptacle where things are stored. Repositories for genealogy records are usually places like courthouses, archives, and the Family History Library. If you are doing online research, the repository is "the internet," but it is more helpful to specify the exact website you are using. For example, *Ancestry, FamilySearch, FreeBMD,* etc.

- **URL, Call #, Film #**: If you are searching online, copy and paste the URL of the record collection. If you are in a library or archive, include the call number or microfilm number.

- **Searching for:** write the names of the people you are looking for and what information you hope to find.
- **Locality:** the location you are searching within, i.e. the county, state, or country you are looking for records.

- **Source:** describe the document or book you are researching within. If you find something, you will edit this section to contain a more exact citation, including page number, etc.

- **Results/Notes:** Describe what you found. If you found nothing, write NIL (not in location).

Search for records

Now that you have a list of the records you want to search, go ahead and look in those collections for the names of the people you are hoping to find. As you go, update your research log.

These are the fields you'll need to update:

- **URL, Call #, Film #** - if you find a record, change the URL to be the specific location of the record for your relative. If the link is very long, you can shorten it using Bitly (https://bitly.com). I have used Bitly to shorten the links in my research log on the next page. The URL is important because it helps you find the record again.

- **Source** - when you find a record, add additional data to your source citation. You may be able to copy and paste the source citation from the website. As you become more advanced, you can learn how to create better source citations. A source citation is important because it tells you how to find the record again and shows others where your information came from. To learn more about creating source citations, see this article:

  "Source citations: The Good, the Bad, and the Ugly" available at *Family Locket*: https://familylocket.com/source-citations-the-good-the-bad-and-the-ugly/

- **Results/Notes** - This is where you record the details you found in the source. You don't need to put everything here, just a few details to remind you of what you found.

Below is a sample research log showing for my Pearce Bradley research project. You will see that I added the dates, results, and updated the URLs.

Research Log						
Objective:		Who are the children of Pearce Sumpter Bradley, born 7 October 1821 to Mary Powderill Bradley in Swineshead, Lincolnshire, England, and married Jane Baldock, 8 February 1849, also in Swineshead?				
Date	Website or Repository	URL, Call #, Film #	Searching for	Locality	Source Citation	Results/Notes
6/19/18	Ancestry	https://search.ancestry.com/search/db.aspx?dbid=8860	Pearce Bradley and Jane	Swineshead, Lincolnshire, England	1851 England Census	NIL (not in location) - There is no Pearce Bradley in Swineshead 1851. Broaden search to include all of England.
6/19/18	Ancestry	https://ancstry.me/2K6Ec50	Pearce Bradley and Jane	England	1851 England Census, New Stranton, Durham, England, Household 28, Piece 2384, Folio 124, Page 8.	Pearce Bradley (30), Mary Jane Bradley (27), Mary Jane Bradley (1), B Bradley (4 mo)
6/19/18	Ancestry	https://ancstry.me/2I2ecTi	Pearce Bradley and Jane	England	1861 England Census, Spittlegate, Lincolnshire, England, Household 195, Piece 2352, Folio 70, Page 28.	Pearce Bradley (37), Jane (35), Mary J (11), Walter B (10), Eliza A (8), Joseph P (6), Henry (3), Emma (1), William P (1/12)
6/19/18	Ancestry	https://ancstry.me/2M6NlYF	Pearce Bradley and Jane	Spittlegate, Lincolnshire, England	1871 England Census, Spittlegate, Lincolnshire, England, Household 60, Piece 3360, Folio 56, Page 10.	Pearce Bradley (50), Jane (46), Mary J (21), Walter (21), Eliza (18), Joseph (16), Henry (13), Emma (11), Frederick (7), Kate (4)
6/19/18	Ancestry	https://ancstry.me/2I2YyXu	Pearce Bradley and Jane	Spittlegate, Lincolnshire, England	1881 England Census, Spittlegate, Lincolnshire, England, Piece 3233, Folio 110, Page 33.	Pearce S. Bradley (59), Jane W. (62), Eliza A. (28), Frederick W. (18), Catherine (14)

6/19/18	Ancestry	https://ancstry.me/2ligdS6	Children of Pearce and Jane Bradley	Spittlegate, Lincolnshire, England	1891 England Census, Grantham, Spittlegate, Lincolnshire, England, Piece 2585, Folio 155, Page 22.	Pearce S. Bradley (70), Jane W. (74), Mary J. (42), Eliza A. (37).
6/19/18	Ancestry	https://search.ancestry.co.uk/search/db.aspx?dbid=1351	Children of Pearce and Jane Bradley	Spittlegate, Lincolnshire, England	England & Wales Christening Index, 1530-1906	NIL - no children of a man named Pearce Bradley in Swineshead. Searched in Lincolnshire, no children of Pearce.
6/19/18	Ancestry	https://ancstry.me/2tlaNJL	Will of Pearce Bradley	Lincolnshire, England	England & Wales, National Probate Calendar, 1858-1966, 1873-1995	Pearce Bradley, death 30 Aug 1896, of Grantham, Lincolnshire, England, Probate 20 Oct 1896 to William Henry Lincoln

Analyze the Records

As you find historical records, analyze them to determine whether they match your ancestor. You should also consider whether the record is accurate.

Matching Records to People

Do the unique identifiers of your relative match the person on the record? They will not always match exactly, because of inaccuracy of records, so don't rule out a record because it does not match exactly.

Do the unique identifiers match?
- Name
- Birth Date
- Birth Place
- Spouse / relative
- Marriage date
- Marriage place
- Death date
- Death place
- Residence

Birthdates that are calculated from ages on census records may not always match up perfectly. Sometimes they can vary 5-10 years. This is because the informant was not always an eyewitness to the birth of the person they are giving the age for, like a spouse. The spouse of a person is a helpful unique identifier but remember that spouses often died and your relative may have remarried. If the transcription seems close but one thing is off, check the original record. It is possible that the handwriting was misinterpreted by the indexer.

Below is an example of matching records to your relative using unique identifiers from my research project to identify Pearce Bradley's children.

Record Matching			
Unique Identifier	Already Known	Possible Record Match: 1851 Census	Notes
Name	Pearce Sumpter Bradley	Pearce Bradley	Same first and last name
Birth year	Baptized 7 Oct 1821	abt 1821	If he was baptized as an infant, this would be correct
Birthplace	Baptized in Swineshead, Lincolnshire, England	Born in Shutterton, Lincolnshire, England	Same county, but how close are Swineshead and Shutterton?
Spouse's name	Jane Baldock	Mary Jane Bradley	Jane is the same, but there is the addition of the first name "Mary." She was married in the 1851 census, so she was going by her husband's surname, Bradley.
Residence	Swineshead, Lincolnshire, England	New Stranton, Durham, England	This is not the expected location of residence. How far away is New Stranton

			from Swineshead?

The name matches as well as the baptism and estimated birth date (calculated from his age on the census). The next three unique identifiers don't match up exactly. Let's go through each one and see what questions to ask as we determine if this census is a match to my relative Pearce Bradley.

- Birthplace - Pearce was baptized in Swineshead. That does not mean that he could not have been born in "Shutterton." Where is "Shutterton?" There is no place called Shutterton in England, but when I look back at my locality information, I notice a parish near Swineshead called Sutterton. This could have been where Pearce was born, since it is close to where his baptism took place

- Spouse's name - We already know that Pearce Bradley married Jane Baldock. After their marriage, Jane would have been known by her married name, Jane Bradley. This is the name I was expecting to see, but on the 1851 census, Pearce's wife is listed as "Mary Jane Bradley." Is this the same person as Jane? It is possible. Perhaps her full name was Mary Jane but she went by Jane.

- Residence - It was unexpected to find Pearce Bradley living somewhere other than Swineshead. However, because I looked at the map of England while gathering locality information prior to my research, I recognize the county of Durham as being only one county away from Lincolnshire. It is about 160 miles away from Swineshead. This seems pretty far, but, there are some other clues on the census that can help determine if this is the same Pearce Bradley from Swineshead or not.

- Additional clues - I looked at the birthplaces of the children on the census. Pearce's daughter, Mary Jane Bradley, was born in Swineshead. This is just the clue I needed to say more certainly that the 1851 Census for Pearce Bradley in New Stranton, Durham, matches my relative, Pearce Bradley of Swineshead, Lincolnshire.

Matching records to your relatives is an important step. Take the time to review each detail in the record for clues. If you are not sure if the record matches, type your thoughts in the notes column of your research log and come back to it later.

If you search all the records in your research log and find nothing to answer your research question, do not be discouraged. Record the date of your search and write a summary of what you did. As you write, you may have new ideas about where to look next.

Determining Accuracy

As you find records, you not only want to determine if it's a match, but how accurate it is.

To determine the accuracy of a record, you will evaluate three things: the source, the information in the source, and how the information applies to your research question (evidence). Here are the questions to ask:

Source: Is this source an original record, derivative record, or an authored narrative?

- *Original source*: the first record created for an event - the actual historical document or image of it, i.e. census, birth certificate, will

- *Derivative source*: a record that was created from another record, i.e. index, transcription, abstract

- *Authored narrative*: a record that an author created by combining analysis of several records, i.e. a family tree published online, a family history book written by a relative, biography of an ancestor

Information: Is the information primary, secondary, or undetermined?

- *Primary*: the informant was an eyewitness to the event they are giving information about

- *Secondary*: the informant was giving secondhand information that they heard from someone else

- *Undetermined*: on most census records, the informant is undetermined because we don't know who was giving the information to the census taker

Evidence: Is the evidence direct, indirect, or negative?

- *Direct*: the evidence directly states the answer to a research question - i.e. the 1851 census in New Stranton answers directly that Pearce Bradley had children and lists their names.

- *Indirect*: The evidence does not directly state the answer to our research question but provides clues that can answer the research question when combined with other evidence and clues. i.e. The search I performed for Pearce Bradley in Swineshead in the 1851 census showed that he did not live there. This search gave me indirect evidence that Pearce Bradley moved and guided me to search elsewhere in 1851 for his family.

- *Negative*: the absence of information where it is expected to be is evidence. i.e. Pearce Bradley's son Walter was absent on the 1881 census. This is negative evidence that he moved, got married or died between 1871 and 1881.

You may want to add three columns for analyzing the source, information and evidence to your timeline spreadsheet and research log spreadsheet.

Below is an example of a research log with columns for analyzing source, information, and evidence.

Research Log for Pearce Sumter Bradley									
Objective:		Who are the children of Pearce Sumter Bradley, christened 7 October 1821 in Swineshead, Lincolnshire, England, son of Mary Powderill Bradley, and married Jane Baldock, 8 February 1849, also in Swineshead?							
Date	Website or Repository	URL, Call #, Film #	Searching for	Locality	Source Citation	Results/ Notes	Source	Information	Evidence
6/19/18	*Ancestry*	https://search.ancestry.com/search/db.aspx?dbid=8860	Pearce Bradley and Jane	Swineshead, Lincolnshire	1851 England Census	NIL (not in location) - There is no Pearce Bradley in Swineshead 1851. Broaden search to include all of England.	Derivative	Primary	Indirect
6/19/18	*Ancestry*	https://ancstry.me/2K6Ec50	Pearce Bradley and Jane	England	1851 England Census, New Stranton, Durham.	Pearce Bradley (30), Mary Jane Bradley (27), Mary Jane Bradley (1), B Bradley (4 mo)	Original	Undetermined	Direct
6/19/18	*Ancestry*	https://ancstry.me/2tlaNJL	Will of Pearce Bradley	Swineshead, Lincolnshire	England & Wales, National Probate Calendar, 1858-1966, 1873-1995	Pearce Bradley, death 30 Aug 1896, of Grantham, Lincolnshire, England, Probate 20 Oct 1896 to William Henry Lincoln	Derivative	Undetermined	Indirect

In the first entry above, my search for Pearce Bradley in Swineshead on the 1851 census turned up nothing. Here is my analysis:

- **Source:** I searched the 1851 England Census database of indexed entries on *Ancestry*, therefore the source was a derivative. If I had read through each census page created in 1851, that would have been an original source.

- **Information:** *Primary* - the informant for the census was the census taker, who was going from house to house and writing down each person's name, therefore he was an eyewitness to the residence of the people in Swineshead, so the information is primary.

- **Evidence:** *Indirect* - for the question, "Who were Pearce Bradley's children," the evidence that they did not live in Swineshead is indirect. The fact that they did not reside in Swineshead does not tell me the names of his children but gives me a clue that can be combined with other clues to help me come to the correct conclusion.

In the second entry, I located Pearce Bradley and his family in New Stranton, Durham, England.

- **Source:** *Original* - I started my search with a derivative record - the indexed entries in Ancestry's database, but when I found the entry for Pearce, I looked at the image of the actual census document created in 1851. Thus, the source is an original.
- **Information:** *Primary and undetermined* - there are several pieces of information to analyze in the census. The informant for the residence was the census taker, so that information is primary. The informant for the

household information, including the names and ages of each family member was likely one of the heads of household - probably Pearce of Mary Jane. We cannot know for sure who the informant was, so the information about household members is undetermined.

- **Evidence**: *Direct* - the information about Pearce's household and family is direct evidence answering research question "Who are Pearce Bradley's children?"

In the third entry, my search for Pearce Bradley in the England and Wales National Probate Calendar Index was successful in locating a probate record for Pearce Bradley in 1896.

- **Source:** *Derivative* - this is an index created from original probate documents. To read the full probate record, I would need to order the file from the Principal Probate Registry in England. This index was created from the original probate, so it is a derivative.

- **Information:** *Undetermined* - the information in the index does not give enough detail about who provided the information to determine the informant.

- **Evidence:** *Indirect* - no information in the index mentions any children of Pearce Bradley - just his death date, residence, occupation, etc. This information is indirect evidence. It does not directly state the names of Pearce Bradley's children and would have to be combined with additional evidence to answer my research question.

After evaluating the source, information, and evidence, you can determine how accurate a record is. The most accurate information is primary information, from an original source, providing direct evidence.

If the record is a derivative, read it with a critical eye. Remember that someone else has read it and could have mis-interpreted the handwriting. Track down the original record if possible and read it yourself.

If the record contains information that is not primary, do not expect the names, dates, and birthplaces to be 100% correct. A person who is relaying secondhand information may not remember each detail accurately.

If the evidence you find is indirect or negative, be sure to take detailed notes and write out your conclusions to help you put the pieces together. You may also come across conflicting evidence. Weigh the reliability of each record by reviewing the source and information, and then choose which evidence is more likely to be accurate.

5

Record Your Findings

Recording what you found is an essential part of the research process. You should record the information in your own notes, your personal genealogy database, like RootsMagic or Family Tree Maker, and *FamilySearch Family Tree.*

When selecting personal genealogy database software, you may want to consider using one that is compatible with *FamilySearch,* like RootsMagic, Ancestral Quest, and Legacy Family Tree.

In the *FamilySearch Family Tree,* other users can view the person page for the relatives you are researching. They will see the information and reason statements you have added. If you do not add reason statements and attach sources, others may not understand your work and may change it.

The collaborative nature of *FamilySearch Family Tree* is another reason why you should keep a record of your conclusions in your own notes and your personal genealogy database. If someone changes what you have added to *FamilySearch,* you will still have your conclusions in your personal files.

There are many ways to record the information you found in the research phase. Write a summary of your research, attach sources, add new information, and add new people to the tree. This chapter will also address merging duplicate profiles in *FamilySearch*.

The best order to record information is whatever order works best for you. When my findings are straightforward, attaching the sources and writing about them as I go works well. But when the evidence is indirect, I write a research report first to help me make conclusions. Then when I feel I have proven the answer to my research question, I add the information to the tree and attach the research report as a document in the memories section of a person page at *FamilySearch.*

Find what works for you, but don't skip writing about what you found and attaching your sources. It's important to share what you find so others don't duplicate your efforts.

Write a Summary of your Research

Writing a summary of what you found may seem redundant when you have a research log. However, if you take a break from your research and come back to it a few months later, reading your research log will be a difficult task. It's much easier to read about what you found in narrative format. The purpose of writing a summary of research is to make sense of what you find and record ideas for the future. This is especially important if you are assembling indirect evidence to make a case about an ancestor's parentage or identity.

There are many forms this writing can take, from a very simple summary in the life sketch in *FamilySearch*, to a research report in which you discuss the evidence in a difficult case.

Life Sketch

If you have found several pieces of direct evidence that match easily with the person you are researching, you may want to write your conclusions in your relative's life sketch on *FamilySearch*. This works well if information is straightforward and simple and doesn't require in-depth explanation.

Research Report

If your research reveals information that requires in-depth analysis, you may want to write a report. This will help you make the connections, share your conclusions with others, and remember where you left off for the next time you research the same family.

Begin a document with your research objective at the top. Go through each item in your research log and state what you found. Analyze the source, information, and evidence. State how the information answers the research question. Discuss conflicting evidence and how all the evidence comes together to form a conclusion. If you cannot form a conclusion, simply write what you found and conclude that more research is needed. At the end, make a list of "future research suggestions" with ideas and questions about what to do next.

Reason Statements

When you make changes to a profile in *FamilySearch Family Tree*, you are asked to give a reason statement. For example, if you change a person's birthdate or place, you will be asked why you are making that change. It is important to write your conclusions in the reason statement box each time you make a change, even if it's just amending the reason statement that you added before. If you attach a source, you will also be asked to provide a reason statement.

For example, when I determined that the 1851 Census of Pearce Bradley in New Stranton matched my relative, Pearce Bradley, I attached the source in *FamilySearch* and used this reason statement:

I believe that the 1851 census for Pearce Bradley in New Stranton matches the Pearce Bradley of Swineshead who married Jane Baldock because his first and last name match, and his birth year calculated from his age on the census matches his baptism date of 1821. The census indicates that he was born in Shutterton [Sutterton], a parish close to Swineshead where he was baptized. Pearce's wife's name on the census record is listed as "Mary Jane," but the marriage record lists her name as just "Jane." Mary Jane is probably her full name. The residence place on this census, New Stranton, Durham, is relatively far away from Pearce and Jane's marriage location of Swineshead, Lincolnshire but Durham borders Yorkshire which borders Lincolnshire to the North. The census lists Pearce and Mary Jane's daughter, Mary Jane Bradley, as being born in Swineshead, a helpful clue that they were married there and then moved to New Stranton.

When I attached the 1851 census to Pearce's wife Jane, I wrote:

I believe that Mary Jane Bradley on the 1851 census of New Stranton, Durham matches Jane Baldock who married Pearce Bradley in 1849 in Swineshead, because the middle names match - the census states "Mary Jane" and the marriage just states "Jane." Mary Jane was probably her full name. Pearce and Jane were married in Swineshead, and then according to the 1851 census, their daughter Mary Jane was born in Swineshead also. Therefore, it is highly probable that this Mary Jane Bradley on the 1851 census with Pearce Bradley is the same Jane Baldock Pearce married in 1849.

When you are making statements of fact in genealogy, it is helpful to use terms that state how certain you are. Here are some examples:

- Almost certain
- Highly probable
- Probable
- Possible
- Not likely

It is rarely possible to state for certain or "definitely" that a genealogical conclusion is accurate. Usually the most certain you can be about a genealogical conclusion is "almost certain."

Notes

Another place to summarize your research is the "Notes" section of a person profile in *FamilySearch*. Choose a title for your note, then write your note. You may want to write a list of sources you looked for but didn't find, or the questions you had when you were finished researching a person. Most personal genealogy databases like PAF or RootsMagic also have sections for you to record notes.

Attach sources

When you determine that a record matches your ancestor, use the *FamilySearch* Source Linker to attach the record to your tree. If you have found information on another website, you can use the *RecordSeek* browser extension to attach the source to your relative's *FamilySearch* profile. This is found at https://recordseek.com. When you use Record Seek to attach sources from other websites, it is helpful to add a transcription of what the record says, or an abstract of the main details.

If you use *Ancestry.com,* you can add sources to your Ancestry tree, then transfer information from your *Ancestry* tree to the *FamilySearch Family Tree* by clicking on the *FamilySearch* icon at the top of a person's profile page at *Ancestry.*

If you find a record in a different online database, you can often find the same record in *FamilySearch's* database as well. If you do this, it will be easier to attach records to the *FamilySearch Family Tree.* Using the Source Linker, you can attach records to the whole family at once. Go to Familysearch.org and click the "Search" tab. Then search for the source that you found elsewhere to see if *FamilySearch* has it also. If you find it, click "attach" and use the Source Linker to attach the record to everyone in the family. When you add sources and information, it is important to fill out the "reason statement" box, as discussed earlier. The Source Linker will copy your reason statement for each person in the record. You can either write the reason statement to apply to all the people in the household, or you can write a new one for each person.

Add New Information and People

While attaching sources in *FamilySearch* with the Source Linker, you can add facts to a person's profile, including residence, birth and death information, and so on. The Source Linker will not overwrite existing information, it will only add information about an event from if that event's information is empty. For example, if you already have a birth year of 1836 for your relative, but you find the exact birth date on a headstone is 2 February 1836, the Source Linker will not overwrite the existing birth year of 1836. You need to go the person page when you are done with the Source Linker and manually change the birth date. Make a note of the information in the record, then update the fact after you attach the source.

Standardized Dates and Places

The standard format for recording dates is day, month spelled out, then year, i.e. 23 July 1902.

The standardized format for recording places is to begin with the smallest jurisdiction and go to the largest. Include the county, state, and country, i.e. Tucson, Pima, Arizona, United States. As you add these dates and place names to *FamilySearch*, you will see that the system suggests standardized information for you. For example, as you type Manchester, you will see a list of standardized place names that include Manchester:

- Manchester, Jamaica
- Manchester, Lancashire England
- Manchester, Mendocino, California, United States
- Manchester Township, Guysborough, Nova Scotia, Canada

There are many place names called Manchester. If the record does not say which Manchester it is, you can use a map, *FamilySearch Wiki,* and *Wikipedia* to help you determine the jurisdictions of a place.

Be sure to select a standardized location when you enter the place of events so *FamilySearch* can make more accurate suggestions for research hints and possible duplicates.

Adding New People

If you have found new people to add to *FamilySearch Family Tree,* go to the person page of the person you were researching and click "add spouse," "add child," or "add parent." To add a new person, you must state if they are male or female, living or deceased, and how they are connected to someone already in the tree.

The *FamilySearch* Source Linker allows you to add new family members found on a record to *Family Tree*. Simply click "add," and the person's details from the record populate the fields on a sidebar pop-up window titled "create new person." You are asked to select whether the person is living or deceased. Only select deceased if they were born more than 110 years ago or you have a source confirming that they are deceased. Then click "Create a New Person." Adding a new person is exciting. This means that you will be able to reserve their temple ordinances, unless you find a duplicate profile. In that case, their temple work may have already been done. More information on finding duplicates and merging will be discussed at the end of this chapter.

Children Under Age 8

Before reserving temple work for children, it's important to confirm that they lived beyond the age of 8. If they died as a child, the only temple work that is needed is sealing to parents.

Here are some clues that a person lived beyond the age of 8:
- They appear on a census and are over age 8
- They were married
- Their death year indicates that they died at an age greater than 8

Here are some clues that a child died before the age of 8:
- They appear on only one census with the family, then they disappear, although they would have been a child or teen on the next census
- There is no record for them after their birth record
- You find a death record for them that shows they died before age 8

You are not required to fill out the birth, marriage, and death dates and places for a person before you can reserve their temple work. However, you should look for these details and then add the most specific information you find. If you find that a person was born in Swineshead, Lincolnshire, England on one record, and the other record says just Lincolnshire, England, be sure to add the more specific location. It is also helpful to add the residence information of a person each census year that you find for them. This information uniquely identifies the person and helps show that they are unique from others with the same name. *FamilySearch* requires the following information to reserve an ordinance for a relative:

- First or last name
- Gender
- Date of birth, christening, marriage, or death
- Place of birth, christening, marriage, or death
- Death status (living or deceased)

Merge Duplicate Profiles

Before you reserve temple work, check *FamilySearch Family Tree* for duplicates that need to be merged. You can do this by clicking "possible duplicates" at the bottom right hand side of a person page in *FamilySearch*. If there are no possible duplicates, then *FamilySearch* will allow you to reserve the temple work.

Sometimes clicking "possible duplicates" is not enough to find the duplicate profiles. To ensure there are no duplicates, find as many sources about a person as possible, fill out their birth and death dates as specifically as possible, and add all their spouses and children to the tree. Merge any duplicates among their spouse and children, then check for possible duplicates again.

Sometimes, during the process of adding information and attaching records, you may find duplicate profiles that need to be merged. A common scenario is that you are searching for a baptism or christening record for a relative born in England and you find a Church of England baptism that matches your relative. You try to attach the record to your relative, but it is already attached to someone else. This could be a duplicate profile that you need to merge with your relative. Write down the name and ID number. If "possible duplicates" doesn't find this duplicate profile, you can "merge by ID" and paste the ID number of the duplicate profile you found.

Do your best to find duplicate profiles before reserving temple ordinances for a person. Duplicating temple work is a problem Church leaders have been trying to solve for several years and is the reason why the *FamilySearch* website was created.

How to Merge Profiles on FamilySearch

Before you do a merge, you should decide if the two profiles match. You can do this with the merging tool. At the end of the merging tool, you can select "cancel" or "not a match," or "merge." To determine if two profiles match, follow the same steps used in Chapter Four when deciding if a record matches your relative. The merging process puts the two profiles next to each other. Compare the details side-by-side. Be sure to check each fact carefully before merging. If you are not certain that the profiles refer to the same person, do not merge them. Do more research first.

If you make a mistake, you can unmerge the profiles by going to the list of recent changes on the person page. However, after a change is made to the merged profile, the merge is much more difficult to undo. Do not merge profiles unless you are almost certain that they are a match.

When merging, everything on the left will be saved when the merge is over, and everything on the right will be deleted. Make sure you add each detail you want to keep from the right over to the left before you click "merge." Choose facts that are more specific to keep. If one fact overwrites another fact with a detail you don't want to lose, write a note and add the detail to the merged profile when done.

In the example of a merge of Mary Clark and Mary below, I need to choose which information to keep for each fact - the information on the left or right. I have already decided these two are a match, because the death dates match, the county of death, Derbyshire, match, and the spouse matches. The other details are close.

Mary Clark	Mary
Born 1836, England	Born Swineshead, Lincolnshire, England
Died 2 June 1892, Derbyshire	Died 2 June 1892, Tideswell, Derbyshire, England
Spouse: John Blincowe ID: L5DX-HC5	Spouse: John Blincowe ID: R3XM-FK3

Which birth information should I keep, the left of the right? I wanted to keep both details, 1836 and Swineshead, Lincolnshire England, but the merge tool requires that you choose one or the other, so I will made a note of the complete birth details in my research notebook: Mary Clark, born 1836, in Swineshead, Lincolnshire England. Then, after the merge, I went to her person page and manually updated her birth details.

Which death information should I keep, the left or the right? I chose the details on the right because they contain a more complete death place.

Which spouse should I keep? Both. The ID numbers are different, so that indicates that I need to merge the two profiles of John Blincowe also. A good rule of thumb is to always add spouses, children, and parents to the merged profile, then no relationships will be lost during the merge.

Merging is a complex process. The more you know about the two people before you merge them, the better. You may need to open their person pages in a new window and review the sources and additional details before you can merge.

At the end of a merge, be sure to add a reason statement clarifying how you know that the two profiles are a match. For example:

These two profiles for Mary Clark are for the same person. This is clear because they have the same spouse and the same death date and same county of death.

Sometimes your explanation will be a bit longer if some of the unique identifiers don't match exactly. For example, when merging Anna Jarvis and Hannah Gibbs, the following was my reason statement:

Anna Jarvis and Hannah Gibbs are the same person. Hannah Gibbs married Henry Jarvis. Her name was recorded as Anna Jarvis in the household of Henry Jarvis in 1871, however her age, children, and birth place in Preston are the same. The census taker could have heard her name pronounced "anna" instead of "Hannah." In subsequent census years, her name is listed as Hannah Jarvis. Therefore, Hannah "Anna" (Gibbs) Jarvis, wife of Henry Jarvis, is one person.

If you feel that merging is a difficult task, you are not alone. President Henry B. Eyring told about his experience with merging two profiles in *FamilySearch* in General Conference.

> "Just a few weeks ago, I was working on my family history with a consultant by my side and another helper on the phone. On the computer screen before me was a problem beyond my mortal power to solve. I saw two names, sent to me by the wonders of technology, of people who might be waiting for a temple ordinance. But the trouble was that the names were different, but there was a reason to believe they might be the same person. My task was to determine what was true.
>
> I asked my consultants to tell me. They said, "No, you must choose." And they were completely sure I would discover the truth. The computer, with all its power and information, had left me the blessing of staring at those names on a screen, evaluating the available information, seeking other research, praying silently, and discovering what was true. As I prayed, I knew with surety what to do—just as I have in other situations when I needed to rely on heaven's help to solve a problem."[7]

As you research, weigh the information, and pray, I am confident you will be guided as you merge duplicate profiles.

---

[7] Henry B. Eyring, "Gathering the Family of God," April 2017 General Conference talk, article online, *LDS.org* (www.lds.org/general-conference : accessed 28 June 2018).

6

Reserve Temple Ordinances

Now that you have added new relatives to *FamilySearch Family Tree,* attached sources, and ensured there are no duplicates, you are ready to reserve temple ordinances. The temple ordinance tab in a person profile allows you to do this.

Go to the person page of the relative whose work you want to reserve. Click "Ordinances." There you will see a list of the ordinances that need to be completed. If there is enough information about your relative, the temple icons will be green and say "Request." Click "Request" and select which ordinances you would like to reserve.

Church Policies for Temple Work

After clicking request, you will be prompted to review the church policies for proxy temple work. Review these each time you reserve temple ordinances. The policies for temple work, as of 2018, include:

"Temple ordinances are sacred and should be treated with respect. Please reserve ordinances for individuals only if you are related to them.

Who You Can Do Ordinances For

You are responsible to submit names of the following individuals:
1. Immediate family members
2. Direct-line ancestors (parents, grandparents, great-grandparents, and so on, and their families).

You may also submit the names of the following individuals:
1. Biological, adoptive, and foster family lines connected to your family.
2. Collateral family lines (uncles, aunts, cousins, and their families).
3. Descendants of your ancestors.
4. Your own descendants.
5. Possible ancestors, meaning individuals who have a probable family relationship that cannot be verified because the records are inadequate, such as those who have the same last name and resided in the same small geographic area as your known ancestors.

Do not submit the following individuals unless you are related to them:
1. Famous people.
2. Those gathered from unapproved extraction projects.
3. Jewish Holocaust victims. Members can do the ordinances for these people only under the following conditions:
   a. They are an immediate family member of the deceased (defined as parents, spouse, children or siblings).
   b. Or they have permission of all living immediate family members.
   c. Or they have the permission of the closest living relative if no immediate family members are living.

Persons Born within the Last 110 Years

To do ordinances for a deceased person who was born in the last 110 years, the following requirements must be met.

1. The person must have been deceased for at least one year.
2. You must either be one of the closest living relatives, or you must obtain permission from one of the closest living relatives. If you are not a spouse, child, parent, or sibling of the deceased, please obtain permission from one of the closest living relatives before doing the ordinances. The closest living relatives are an undivorced spouse (the spouse to whom the individual was married when he or she died), an adult child, a parent, or a brother or sister. Verbal approval is acceptable. Family members should work together to determine when the ordinances will be done and who will do them."[8]

You should only reserve as many temple ordinances as you can complete within two years. After that time, the ordinances may be unreserved for other users to request.

Print Ordinance Cards

When you are ready to go to the temple and perform the ordinances for your relatives, there are two ways to print the names you have reserved. You can print a Family Ordinance Request to take to the temple office. They will take the request, print the cards, and cut them for you at the temple. The other option is to print the temple cards yourself. All you need is plain white paper.

Go to the "Temple" Tab of *FamilySearch* to see the list of names you have reserved. Check the boxes next to the names you would like to print. Choose which ordinances you want to do, then click print. A PDF will be generated which you can print or save for later. Print the cards on white paper, then cut them out.

---

[8] "Who You Can Do Work For," policies for temple Work, notice online, *FamilySearch Family Tree* (www.familysearch.org : accessed 28 June 2018).

Share Ordinances

If you would like to share temple ordinances with someone else, go to the temple tab, check the box next to the relatives you would like to share, and click "share" at the top. You can choose between sharing with the temple or sharing with family or friends.

To share with family or friends, you must enter their name and their email address. They will receive a notification from *FamilySearch* that they have received a name for the temple from you. They will be prompted to click the link and accept the name. It will then be added to their *FamilySearch* account and appear in their temple list and they can print the ordinance cards themselves.

7

Repeat the Process

When you have completed the entire process, you may want to find additional names for the temple. Go back to beginning of the process and repeat the steps.

If you did not find any new relatives to add to the tree, don't despair. This does not mean your time was wasted. You kept a log of where you searched, and you wrote a summary of what you learned. Now you can move on to a new research question. You may want to continue researching the same person, or you may be ready to move on to another candidate.

If your tree is full and you're doing descendancy research, you have a long list of ancestors to use as starting points for descendancy research. You have already found candidates for further research within their descendancy trees. Select another one of these candidates and repeat the research process.

Choose a New Research Question

When it's time to choose a new research question, you might want to choose a question that focuses on the same person. Maybe you found their spouse and now you want to find their children. Be sure to update your research objective with any new identifiers you have found. Before you start, reread your last research report or notes. From those notes, you may have ideas for what to do next. An important part of professional genealogy research is including a list of future research suggestions in the report. This allows you to pick up your research right where you left off, even if you come back several weeks or months later.

If you found the parents of an ancestor in your last project, you may now want to search for their marriage date in your next project.

As you become proficient using the research method in Chapter Four, you may decide to take on a challenging project to prove a relationship in the more distant past. Maybe one of your 5th great grandparents in New England has no parents. Find out what records are available for that time and place and make a research plan. Search the records and see what you can find. Remember that any time spent researching is not wasted if you keep a research log and write a summary of what you learned, even if you found nothing.

Next Steps in Descendancy Research

If you are doing descendancy research, and your previous research question focused on one of the children of a large family, you may now want to turn your attention to one of the other children in the family. Eventually, you can research all the children in the family and find all the grandchildren of a particular ancestral couple. Next, you can find all their great-grandchildren. Generally, in each generation, the number of descendants increases.

After you have completed researching all the descendants of the ancestors in your list, you are ready to go back one more generation. Create a new list of ancestors as starting points for descendancy research with the *parents* of the ancestors in your previous list.

Remember that the connection between you and the ancestor should be reviewed for accuracy before embarking on descendancy research. You may need to do a research project to prove the relationship between an ancestor and his or her parents before you can proceed with descendancy research for that generation.

Save Locality Information

As you complete several projects in the same locality, you may want to save the information you're finding about the history, geography, and available records for a particular county, state, or country. Consider creating a locality guide to keep track of all the places online and offline that you have used to find information, maps, record collections, and other resources.

Involving Others

To share the work that you're doing with other people in your family, consider creating a shared folder in Dropbox or Google Drive. I use Google Drive and often create spreadsheets using Google Sheets to share research ideas with my family who are interested in collaborating. I store my timelines, research logs, and research reports in these online folders to access from multiple devices and share them with family members.

You may have a family member who wants to help but doesn't know where to start. Give them one of the names of the candidates for further research you have identified and a research question to help them get started.

Children and Youth

A good beginning project for children, ages 8-11, and youth, ages 12-18, is to help their parents with reviewing the accuracy of their family tree. They should start with the help of a parent. As children learn how to standardize names, dates, and places, they may be able to do this alone. Parents should check the work of their children.

Another way for children to help parents review the accuracy of the family tree is to look for direct ancestors who have no sources attached and make a list of their names and ID numbers. Parents can then attach record hints or begin a research project to prove the relationship between the ancestor and their parents. Older children, with the help of a parent, may be able to learn how to attach a record hint to an ancestor and determine if it matches. Determining if a record matches can be difficult and should be done with adult guidance several times before attempting independently.

The best way for older children to practice attaching records is with the ancestors closest to them - their grandparents or great-grandparents. They should start with record hints and review each fact carefully to decide if it matches.

Children can help their parents create descendancy trees by using the list the parents have made of ancestors for descendancy research. Children can learn how to create Puzzilla trees and then count the research targets.

Another helpful exercise for beginners is indexing and transcribing familiar records. A beginning level *FamilySearch* indexing project of a common type of genealogical record (i.e. death certificates) is a good starting point. The process of reading and typing the names and dates is helpful for learning basic family history skills. Indexing is good practice for reading handwriting and learning what information is commonly found on each type of record. Children who cannot read cursive can help transcribe headstones at BillionGraves.com.

Census records are a common record that family history researchers use. Children can learn about census records by transcribing census data onto a paper form. The National Archives has printable forms available on their website, www.archives.gov/research/genealogy/charts-forms . Transcription allows children to become familiar with reading handwriting and understanding the information a census contains. Choose a close ancestor, like a grandparent or great-grandparent, and help your child transcribe each fact from one of their census records.

The joy of temple and family history work can be enjoyed by people of all ages, from children to adults, if they learn how to correctly analyze the information in original records and match it to known information.

Small and Simple Things

Knowing where to start is often the biggest obstacle beginners to family history work encounter. This doesn't have to be an obstacle for you anymore. You are now equipped with the knowledge you need find opportunities for research, perform descendancy research, and complete a research project.

This method will always give you a feeling of success and accomplishment, even if you don't find new names for the temple, because you are always making progress - creating lists, checking people off your lists, creating research plans, executing research plans, and writing summaries. By small and simple things, great things are accomplished.

Spend a little time working each day. And remember, this is a spiritual work. You can receive help from the other side of the veil. As you do the work that is required to discover relatives who need temple ordinances, you will be guided from above and will be able to accomplish great things.

Appendix

To download full-sized versions of these charts, go to
https://FamilyLocket.com/FindNames

List of Ancestors for Descendancy Research

Ancestors of:				
Name and birth year	ID	Notes (Birth Year, etc.)	# of Targets in 4 generations	Candidates for Further Research

List of Nonmember Ancestors for Descendancy Research

Nonmember Ancestors of:				
Name	ID	Notes (Spouses names, children who joined the Church)	# of Targets in 4 generations	Candidates for Further Research

Appendix

Timeline

Timeline for:				
Objective:				
Event	Date	Place	Source	Notes

Research Log

Research Log for:						
Objective:						
Date	Website or Repository	URL, Call #, Film #	Searching for	Locality	Source Citation	Results/Notes

Research Log with Evidence Analysis Columns

Research Log									
Objective:									
Date	Website or Repository	URL, Call #, Film #	Searching for	Locality	Source Citation	Results/ Notes	Source	Information	Evidence

Index

Index

S

T

U

W

Made in the USA
Monee, IL
23 July 2023